Natasha Alexandrova

Anna Watt

Прописи
Russian Handwriting

Cover by Natalia Illarionova

http://russianstepbystep.com/

First Edition
Russian Handwriting

Russian Step By Step

ISBN-13: 978-0-9823042-8-0

ISBN-10: 0-9823042-8-5

Printed in the United States of America

Table of Contents

Предисловие

Умение писать от руки – это часть русской культуры. Все люди в России используют прописи в школе и пишут от руки почти каждый день: от писем и открыток, до всякого рода записей (список покупок, конспект лекции, записки, кроссворды, и т.д.). Если у вас есть сомнения, нужно ли учиться писать от руки в наш компьютерный век, мы говорим твёрдое – да! Почерк каждого человека уникален. Более того, он отражает характер человека. Ведь недаром существует графология – наука о почерке. Графология утверждает, что почерк отражает внутренний мир человека больше, чем слова, которые он пишет.

В этой рабочей тетради обратите внимание на следующее:

❖ Порядок написания элементов букв обозначен стрелками. Чтобы научиться писать правильно и быстро, очень важно ему следовать.
❖ Практикуйте не только написание букв, но и их соединений.
❖ Независимо от того правша вы или левша, необходимо наклонять буквы вправо.
❖ Используйте пустые разлинованные страницы в конце тетради для работы с наиболее сложными для вас буквами.

Мы выражаем свои мысли в словах, а слова – в почерке.

Introduction

Handwriting is beautiful and unique. It has personality. If you are wondering whether or not to learn it, we definitely say – do it! Handwriting is a part of Russian culture. All Russians study cursive at school and use it on a daily basis: from writing letters and postcards to jotting down shopping lists or taking notes. Furthermore, you have probably heard that handwriting also reflects your inner self and might say about the person more than the words themselves.

In this workbook we would like you to pay attention to:

❖ The order of the strokes. It is important once you have to write quickly.
❖ Practice not only the letters themselves but also the connections between them.
❖ Whether you are right or left-handed, it's necessary to incline the letters to the right.
❖ Use the empty pages at the back of the book to master the challenging letters.

Мы выражаем свои мысли в словах, а слова – в почерке. *

(We express our thoughts in words, and our words in handwriting.)

Русский Алфавит

А а *Аа*   Б б *Бб*   В в *Вв*   Г г *Гг*

Д д *Дд*   Е е *Ее*   Ё ё *Ёё*   Ж ж *Жж*

З з *Зз*   И и *Ии*   Й й *Йй*   К к *Кк*

Л л *Лл*   М м *Мм*   Н н *Нн*   О о *Оо*

П п *Пп*   Р р *Рр*   С с *Сс*   Т т *Тт*

У у *Уу*   Ф ф *Фф*   Х х *Хх*   Ц ц *Цц*

Ч ч *Чч*   Ш ш *Шш*   Щ щ *Щщ*   Ъ ъ *ъ*

ы *ы*   ь *ь*   Э э *Ээ*   Ю ю *Юю*

Я я *Яя*

А А А А   а а а

А А А А А А А А А А А А А А А А

А

а а а а а а а а а а а а а а а а а

а

Аа

М М М М   м м м м

М М М М М М М М М М М

м м м м м м м м м м м м м м м м

Мм

Мама

мама

П П П П⃗   n n n⃗

П П П П П П П П П П П

П

n n n n n n n n n n n n

n

Пn

Па

Ап

ап

Ам

Папа

папа

л Л Л л л л

л л л л л л л л л л л л л л

л

л л л л л л л л л л л л л л л

Лл

Лл

Лп

лапа

лама

Алла

лампа

O   *(O)*   *o*   *(o)*

O *OOOOOOOOOOOOOOOOO*

O

o *ooooooooooooooooooo*

Oo

по

лом

Поло

пол

Лом

мол

Мало

алло

К Ж Ж К̲ к к к̲ к̲

К К К К К К К К К К К К К К К

К

к к к к к к к к к к к к к к к

к

Кк

Полка

палка

лак

молоко

Кока-кола

комок

мак

14

С С С   с с

С СССССССССССССССССС

с ссссссссссссссссссссс

Сс

сок

Сокол

ласка

Маска

сопка

каска

Колос

коса

оса

Т М Т Т Т т т т т

Т Т Т Т Т Т Т Т Т Т Т

Т

т т т т т т т т т т т т

т

Тт

Том

стол

кто

салат

кот

мост

тост

16

Э Э Э   э Э э

Э з з з з з з з з з з з з з з з з

Э

э э э э э э э э э э э э э э э э э э

э

Ээ

поэт

Это сок.

Это паста.

Это томат.

Д Д Д Д д д д д

Д ДДДДДДДДДДДДДД

Д

д ддддддддддддддд

д

Дд

лодка

дама

мода

Это дом? Да, это дом.

Это доска? Да, это доска.

Н Ж Ж Ж н нн н н

Н Н Н Н Н Н Н Н Н Н Н Н Н Н Н

Н

н н н н н н н н н н н н н н н н

н

Нн

сон

слон

нота

носок

стакан

Это Нонна, а это Том.

З З З   з з з з

З З З З З З З З З З З З З З З

З

з з з з з з з з з з з з з з з

з

Зз

Замок

Сказка

поза

Это знак.

Это зона.

Э Э Э   е е

Э Э Э Э Э Э Э Э Э Э Э Э Э Э Э Э Э Э Э

Э

е е е е е е е е е е е е е е е е е е е

Ээ

Это зонт? Нет, это не зонт.

тема

еда

лес

тесто

Елена ела кекс.

И И И   и и и

И ИИИИИИИИИИИИ

И

и иииииииииииииии

и

Ии

Инна

или

капитан

То Нина или Мила?

То Нина.

Ч Ч Ч ч ч

Ч ч ч ч ч ч ч ч ч ч ч ч ч ч ч

Ч

ч ч ч ч ч ч ч ч ч ч ч ч ч ч ч

ч

Чч

пчела

чек

Инна читает.

Анна – чемпионка.

Что это?

Б Б Б Б б б б

Б б б б б б б б б б б б б

Б

б б б б б б б б б б б б б б б

б

Бб

Бобик

Балет

Банк

билет

Это не кот, это собака.

У У У У У у у у

У у у у у у у у у у у у у у у у у у у

У

у у у у у у у у у у у у у у у у у у у у

у

Уу

чудо

куб

туча

туман

стул

суп

ум

ф ф ф ф   ф ф ф ф

ф ᵠᵖ ᵠᵖ ᵠᵖ ᵠᵖ ᵠᵖ ᵠᵖ ᵠᵖ ᵠᵖ ᵠᵖ ᵠᵖ ᵠᵖ

ф

ф ф ф ф ф ф ф ф ф ф ф ф ф ф

ф

Фф

Фото

офис

кофе

факт

фокус

Это Филипп.

В В В В в в в в

В

В

в

Вв

слово

воск

свет

Валентин

Что это? Это квас.

Это ваза.

Г П Г→   г г̂ г

Г Г

Г

г г

Гг

сигнал

Глеб

год

гвоздика

геолог

Где книга? Вот она.

Галина

Я Я Я Я   я я я я

ЯЯЯЯЯЯЯЯЯЯЯЯЯЯЯ

Я

я яяяяяяяяяяяяяяяя

Яя

Италия

Голубика – синяя ягода.

Япония

мяч

яблоко

Я Ваня. А я Костя.

Р Р Р⃗   р р р⃗

Р ррррррррррррррр

Р

р ррррррррррррррр

р

Рр

мандарин

Сестра Рита

Роберт

Это балерина или доктор?

Роман играет в регби.

Ж Ж Ж Ж ж ж ж ж

Ж Ж Ж Ж Ж Ж Ж Ж Ж

Ж

ж ж ж ж ж ж ж ж ж ж ж

ж

Жж

жираф

живот

массаж

жук

муж и жена

Женя моя сестра.

Ё Ё Ё Ё ё ё ё

Ё Ё Ё Ё Ё Ё Ё Ё Ё Ё Ё Ё Ё Ё

Ё

ё ё ё ё ё ё ё ё ё ё ё ё ё ё

Ёё

Жёлтый клён

ёж

Семён

лёд

Полёт на самолёте

Весёлый Лёва

Й Й Й Й́ й й й́ й́

Й Й Й Й Й Й Й Й Й Й Й Й Й Й Й Й Й

Й

й й й й й й й й й й й й й й й й й

Йй

май

герой

йогурт

майка

Григорий – мой директор.

Это мой чай.

$\mathcal{X}$ $\mathcal{X}$ $\mathcal{X}$ x $\hat{x}$ x

$\mathcal{X}$ $\mathcal{X}$ $\mathcal{X}$ $\mathcal{X}$ $\mathcal{X}$ $\mathcal{X}$ $\mathcal{X}$ $\mathcal{X}$ $\mathcal{X}$ $\mathcal{X}$ $\mathcal{X}$ $\mathcal{X}$

$\mathcal{X}$

x x x x x x x x x x x x x

x

$\mathcal{X}x$

$\mathcal{X}$леб

ухо

холл

Холодно!

Играйте в хоккей!

Ц Ц Ц Ц Ц Ц Ц Ц

Ц Ц Ц Ц Ц Ц Ц Ц Ц Ц Ц Ц Ц Ц

Ц

ц ц ц ц ц ц ц ц ц ц ц ц ц ц ц

ц

Цц

цирк

Пицца

молодец

информация

Мне нужен рецепт.

ь   ь   ь)

ь ь ь ь ь ь ь ь ь ь ь ь ь ь ь ь ь ь ь

ь

соль

Нью-Йорк

семья

конь

ъ   ъ   ъ   ъ)

ъ ъ ъ ъ ъ ъ ъ ъ ъ ъ ъ ъ ъ ъ ъ ъ ъ

ъ

съедобный

въезд

подъезд

Ш Ш Ш Ш ш ш ш ш

Ш Ш Ш Ш Ш Ш Ш Ш Ш Ш Ш Ш

ш ш ш ш ш ш ш ш ш ш ш ш

Шш

бабушка

Шура

шишка

шум

тишина

шоколад

Ты спешишь.

Пиши красиво – не спеши.

Щ Щ Щ Щ Щ   щ щ щ щ щ

Щ Щ Щ Щ Щ Щ Щ Щ Щ Щ

Щ

щ щ щ щ щ щ щ щ щ щ щ

щ

Щщ

борщ

Это щи или борщ?

женщина

щука

Чьи это вещи?

Ю Ю Ю Ю   ю ю ю ю

Ю Ю Ю Ю Ю Ю Ю Ю Ю Ю Ю

Ю

ю ю ю ю ю ю ю ю ю ю ю ю ю ю

ю

Юю

юг

Юлия

вьюга

парашют

Юрий

Я люблю наш парк.

ы ◦ы бы ый

ы ы ы ы ы ы ы ы ы ы ы ы ы ы

ы

мы

рыба

цветы

красные розы

Голубые рыбы

сыновья

сёстры

выход

мыло

Russian Step By Step learning system is designed by an experienced teacher and language course developers to introduce a step-by-step approach to learning Russian. Our goal is to provide the learners of Russian with clear and simple explanations and lots of practice.

For a complete list of titles, prices, more information about our company and learning materials or to subscribe to our free newsletter, please, visit our website at **www. russianstepbystep.com**

If you are teaching Russian using our materials, please contact us regarding a complimentary training at **info@russianstepbystep.com**

Available Titles

1. **Reading Russian Workbook**: Total Beginner (Book & Audio)

2. **Beginner** Level 1 (Book & Audio)

3. **Low Intermediate** Level 2 (Book & Audio)

4. **Intermediate** Level 3 (Book & Audio)

5. Russian Handwriting 1: **Propisi 1**

6. Russian Handwriting 2: **Propisi 2**

7. Russian Handwriting 3: **Propisi 3**

8. **Verbs of Motion**: Workbook 1

9. **Verbs of Motion**: Workbook 2

Children's Series: Age 3 – 7

1. Azbuka 1: **Coloring Russian Alphabet:** Азбука-раскраска (Step 1)

2. Azbuka 2: **Playing with Russian Letters:** Занимательная азбука (Step2)

3. Azbuka 3: **Beginning with Syllables:** Мои первые слоги (Step 3)

4. Azbuka 4: **Continuing with Syllables:** Продолжаем изучать слоги (Step 4)

5. **Animal Names and Sounds:** Кто как говорит Part 1

6. **Animal Names and Sounds: Coloring Book:** Кто как говорит Part 2

7. Propisi for Preschoolers 1: **Russian Letters: Trace and Learn:** Тренируем пальчики (Step 1)

You can also follow us on Facebook **www.facebook.com/RussianStepByStep**

Children's Series: Age 8 - 14

1. **Workbook 1:** Reading Russian Step By Step for Children (Book & Audio)
2. **Teacher's Manual 1**: Russian Step By Step for Children
3. **Student Book 2:** Russian Step By Step for Children (Book & Audio)
4. **Teacher's Manual 2:** Russian Step By Step for Children
5. **Workbook 3:** Reading Russian Step By Step for Children (Book & Audio)
6. **Teacher's Manual 3**: Russian Step By Step for Children
7. **Workbook 4:** Reading Russian Step By Step for Children (Book & Audio)
8. **Teacher's Manual 4**: Russian Step By Step for Children
9. **Workbook 5:** Reading Russian Step By Step for Children (Book & Audio)
10. **Teacher's Manual 5**: Russian Step By Step for Children
11. Russian Handwriting 1: **Propisi 1**
12. Russian Handwriting 2: **Propisi 2**
13. Russian Handwriting 3: **Propisi 3**

Made in the USA
Middletown, DE
22 September 2018